METACOGNITION AFFECTS IN ENHANCING STUDENT'S LEARNING

AZEEM AKTHAR
Farzana Zafar
Javaria Afzal

METACOGNITION AFFECTS IN ENHANCING STUDENT'S LEARNING

METACOGNITION AND LEARNING

VDM Verlag Dr. Müller

Impressum/Imprint (nur für Deutschland/ only for Germany)

Bibliografische Information der Deutschen Nationalbibliothek: Die Deutsche Nationalbibliothek verzeichnet diese Publikation in der Deutschen Nationalbibliografie; detaillierte bibliografische Daten sind im Internet über http://dnb.d-nb.de abrufbar.

Alle in diesem Buch genannten Marken und Produktnamen unterliegen warenzeichen-, marken- oder patentrechtlichem Schutz bzw. sind Warenzeichen oder eingetragene Warenzeichen der jeweiligen Inhaber. Die Wiedergabe von Marken, Produktnamen, Gebrauchsnamen, Handelsnamen, Warenbezeichnungen u.s.w. in diesem Werk berechtigt auch ohne besondere Kennzeichnung nicht zu der Annahme, dass solche Namen im Sinne der Warenzeichen- und Markenschutzgesetzgebung als frei zu betrachten wären und daher von jedermann benutzt werden dürften.

Coverbild: www.ingimage.com

Verlag: VDM Verlag Dr. Müller GmbH & Co. KG
Dudweiler Landstr. 99, 66123 Saarbrücken, Deutschland
Telefon +49 681 9100-698, Telefax +49 681 9100-988
Email: info@vdm-verlag.de

Herstellung in Deutschland:
Schaltungsdienst Lange o.H.G., Berlin
Books on Demand GmbH, Norderstedt
Reha GmbH, Saarbrücken
Amazon Distribution GmbH, Leipzig
ISBN: 978-3-639-32318-4

Imprint (only for USA, GB)

Bibliographic information published by the Deutsche Nationalbibliothek: The Deutsche Nationalbibliothek lists this publication in the Deutsche Nationalbibliografie; detailed bibliographic data are available in the Internet at http://dnb.d-nb.de.

Any brand names and product names mentioned in this book are subject to trademark, brand or patent protection and are trademarks or registered trademarks of their respective holders. The use of brand names, product names, common names, trade names, product descriptions etc. even without a particular marking in this works is in no way to be construed to mean that such names may be regarded as unrestricted in respect of trademark and brand protection legislation and could thus be used by anyone.

Cover image: www.ingimage.com

Publisher: VDM Verlag Dr. Müller GmbH & Co. KG
Dudweiler Landstr. 99, 66123 Saarbrücken, Germany
Phone +49 681 9100-698, Fax +49 681 9100-988
Email: info@vdm-publishing.com

Printed in the U.S.A.
Printed in the U.K. by (see last page)
ISBN: 978-3-639-32318-4

Table of Contents

CHAPTER 1

INTRODUCTION

Life is a continuous process of learning. In spite of various factors, Cognition plays key role in learning and one must know, understand what He /she is learning and getting through senses. This process is called metacognition. Flavell, (1999) continued that Metacognition refer to "Cognition about cognition or knowing about knowing. Metacognitive skills are generally divided into two types: Self assessment &Self management. Self Assessment (the ability to assess one's own cognition), Self management refers to the ability to manage one's further cognitive development.

We engage in metacognitive activities every day. Metacognition consists of both metacognitive knowledge and metacognitive experiences .Metacognitive knowledge refers to acquired knowledge about Cognitive process, knowledge that can be used to control cognitive process Flavell further divides metacognitive knowledge into three categories.

- Knowledge of person variables.
- Knowledge of task variables.
- Knowledge of strategy variables

Knowledge of person variables deals with knowing about oneself and other thinking task variables are concerned with different types of task exert different types of cognitive demands strategy variables or knowledge about cognitive and metacognitive strategies for enhancing learning and performance.

Recent research highlights the importance of metacognitive knowledge and Skill in improving learning. Research has identified various aspects of Metacognition. Two major aspect are; First Social and Emotional and Second is Self Regulating. Self regulation in terms of" process of continuously, monitoring Progress towards a goal. Checking outcomes and redirecting unsuccessful efforts.

3

Self regulatory learning consists of the self generation and self monitoring of thoughts, feelings and behaviors to reach a goal. Self regulatory activities involves such as setting specific goals, self monitoring their learning and systematically evaluating their progress towards a goal. It also involves using various techniques for regulation of behavior such as self reinforcement and self punishment and these techniques are very useful in improving one's learning. Social emotional aspect provides us a comprehensive model with in developmental framework. As students are faced with a difficult situation, they experience success and failure .They receives feedback, occurring frequency, develop into habit attribution of success and failure. Metacognition enables us to be successful learners and has been associated with intelligence. Metacognitive involves active control over the Cognitive process engaged in learning. Metacognitive plays vital role in learning. Successful learners employ a range of metacognitive skill and effective teachers of students attend to develop there skill. This study is related to metacognition & its role in enhancing students learning through extensive review.

1.1 Statement of the Problem

The purpose of this study is to investigate the role of metacognition in enhancing students learning.

1.2 Objective of the Study

a: To identify the role of metacognition in enhancing learning.

b: To determine the role of metacognition in learning.

c: To track out the development of metacognation as a contrast.

d: To identify the role of self regulation I mtacognation.

e: To explore the concept of self regulation.

1.3 Methodology

The study is literature based the researcher reviewed the book, articles, journals, magazine, newspaper, encyclopedia, and these to find out related material about the effectiveness of meta-Cognition.

1.4   Significance of the Study

Metacognitiative can be said as the knowledge about knowledge. It can be very useful in enhancement of learning. It can help a teacher to consolidate student's learning. It can also helpful to students and their cognitive process to learn more. Curriculum planners can seek guidance from this and can develop curriculum according to the Students need.

1.5   Operational Definitions of Key Term

1.6.1   Metacognition

According to Flavell (1999) metacognition means "Cognitions about cognitions" or "knowing about knowing".

1.6.2   Regulation

According to Laura (1999) self-regulation is the process of continually monitoring progress towards a goal checking Outcomes and redirecting and unsuccessful efforts

CHAPTER 2

REVIEW OF RELATED LITERATURE

Metacognition play a vital role in learning. It is the most important for the improving of student's learning. It develops higher order thinking in students. Through metacognition we can know about our mental approach and its levels. Critical age of development of cognition is to 7 to 8 year. Metacognition is a process in which we improve the idea that develops most effective thinking and awareness. In which we change our idea and affect on other task that we create or select. Metacognition refers to awareness and understanding of various aspect of thought.

2.1   Definition of Metacognition

Metacognition means "Cognition about cognitions: or "Knowing about knowing". Flavell (1999).

For Flavell (1995) an awareness & understanding of one's own cognition process. Metacognition involves the planning, monitoring and evaluation of cognitive strategies. Younger children who looks an awareness of their capabilities than they misunderstand others; they might fail to recognize their own errors. It is only when metacognitive abilities become more develop that children are able to know when they don't understand. Such increase reflects a change in their knowledge and believes about the way their mind operates.

Metacognition refers to a level of thinking that connects active control over the procedure of thinking that is used in learning situations. Setting up the way to approach a learning assignment, monitoring conception, and calculating the progress towards the completion of a task: these are skills that are metacognitive in their nature. Likewise, maintaining motivation to see a task to completion is also a metacognitive skill. The capability to become aware of distracting stimuli – both internal and external – and maintain attempt over time also involves metacognitive or executive functions. The theory that metacognition has a vital role to play in successful learning means it is important that it be demonstrated by both students and teachers. Students who demonstrate a wide range of metacognitive skills perform better on exams and complete work more capably. They are self-regulated learners who employ the "right tool for the job" and adjust learning strategies and skills based on their knowledge of effectiveness. Individuals with a high level of metacognitive knowledge and skill classify blocks to learning as early as possible and change "tools" or strategies to ensure goal achievement. The metacognologist is aware of their own strengths and weaknesses, the nature of the task at hand, and accessible "tools" or skills. A broader repertoire of "tools" also assists in goal attainment. When "tools" are general, common, and context independent, they are more likely to be useful in different types of learning situations.

A further feature in metacognition is administrative management and strategic knowledge. Administrative management processes involve planning, monitoring, evaluating and revising one's own thinking processes and products. Strategic knowledge involves knowing what (factual or declarative knowledge), knowing when and why (conditional or contextual knowledge) and knowing how (procedural or methodological knowledge). Both executive management and strategic knowledge metacognition are needed to self-regulate one's own thinking and learning (Hartman, 2001).

According to Wode (1997) metacognition refers to knowledge of one's cognitive abilities. For every type of cognition Metacognition develops substantially over middle childhood. Although pre-school children are totally unaware of what they know and how they perform on certain tasks. He further explains that their abilities increased considerably by 10 to 11 years of age. For example it is not until about 7 to 8 years those children understand the importance of selective attention (attends only to relevant information and ignore irrelevant information).

Similarly children understand of their own memory abilities to evaluate that performance on memory and problem-solving is relatively poor early in childhood but improve substantially by age 11 to 12 years also children are more likely to learn and journalize stages that thoughts to them when there is a significant metacognition competent.

Metacognition can be defined broadly as "any Knowledge or cognitive activity or task as it objects, or regulates, any aspect of any cognitive enterprise" Flaves (1985).

2.1.1   Metacognition and Metaconsciousness

The development of metaconsciousness relies on a progress capacity to engage in conscious and deliberate self-awareness while undertaking important cognitive and personal tasks, they may promote. For Wigfield & Schiefele (1998) one has capabilities, needed for success at the task and of whether one knows how to be a successful at the task.

Bouffard-Bouchard & Pinard (1998) conducted a study designed to examine the degree to which an individual's experimentally induced judgment about their cognitive resources may modulate and affect both their success and failure on the cognitive task and overall management of the resources allocated to the completion of this task. College students were instructed to complete various concept formation problems constructed in such a way that the students would be unable to determine the correctness of their answers. Hence, some students where convinced that they had done very poorly when in fact they had succeeded while others were convinced that they had done very well when in fact they had actually failed the task. Radical differences were observed between the two groups not only in their performance on other equivalent tasks but also in the way that they managed their cognitive resources. The results depicted that for students with the same initial level of ability, these were induced to believe that they had failed, hence with an induced level of low self efficiency, tended to plan their work more poorly, were less Persistent in their efforts to find a solution to the problem presented and appeared less certain of their successes and failures.

Second condition required for an individual's "functional automation is a freedom that risk paralyzing intellectual development. This condition makes references to the fact that even for extremely simple tasks and also for more complex tasks, one may become fully automated at a task but it important to be aware of the steps involved in a particular behavior and to be mindful of one's performance on the task Langer (1992). Otherwise it becomes impossible to avoid sinking into sterilizing and often dangerous routine which limits the possibility constructive and Innovative self-management.

The second level of metaconsciousness consists of an ever increasing capacity for personal and social commitment which refers to higher form of consciousness that allows one to explicitly state the direction one wishes to give to one's personal and social life (Cantor & Harlow, 1994; Ferri & Mahalingham, 1998). Such metaconscious personal and social, commitment is not innate but rather is learned progressively through a conscious reflection that is both affective and intellectuals. However, they may also be unlearned and above all contaminated by motivations, that to say the least, are not always crystal clear.

It is this clarity, this transparence to one's self to others that constitutes the third level; of metaconsciousness. Transparence allows one to gain an even deeper access to what Harter (1998) calls one's authentic self, an access that is important to feeling fulfilled and satisfied with one's action and one's self. These three levels, according to Pinnard (1991), individual to be a far more autonomous, committed and transparent self-management of their cognitive, effective and social life.

2.2.   COMPONENTS OF METACOGNITION

Metacognition include metacognitive experience, things that happen to you that happen to you that pertain to you knowledge or understanding of your own metacognitive process. According to Flavell's (19985) idea is that older children, adults are better able to recognize, and realize the significance of different Meta-cognitive experience. Some psychologist says that younger child perform more poorly on metacognitive task may be they don't have metacognitive knowledge about what the task demands. It may also be that younger children have less metacognitive control over processing of information. Brown (1983). Markman (1979) for instance, showed that 3rd grader were less able than 6th grades to report contradictions in passage that they read even when they read the passage aloud, meta memory is the ability to monitor your own retention is one aspect of metacognition.

Some students however fail to notice when a textbook Contains incomplete information's or when a passage is especially difficult. As a result, they don't study the difficult material, enough and this spend more time then necessary own   material they are ready. (Tavris p.394). Metacognition refers to awareness and understanding of various aspects of thoughts. The information processing system must arrive a such realization. Metacognition refers to one's knowing concerning one's own cognitive process or anything related to them, e.g., the learning relevant properties of information or data. For example, I am engaging in metacognition if I notice that I am having more trouble learning A and B, if it strikes me that I should double check C before accepting is as fact.

Falvell argued that metacognition explains why children of different ages deal with learning tasks in different ways, i.e., they have developed new strategies for thinking. Research studies seem to confirm this conclusion, as children get older they demonstrate more awareness of their thinking process. Metacognition is relevant to work on cognitive styles and learning processes. The work of Piaget is also relevant to research on metacognition since it deals with the development of cognitive in children Gilbert (2002).

Metacognition is one of the latest buzz words in educational Psychology, but what exactly is metacognition? They length and abstract nature of the word makes it sound intimidating, yet is not as daunting a concept as it might seem. We engage in metacognitive activates everyday. Metacognition enables us to be a successful learner, and has been associated with intelligence. (Borkowski, Carr, and Pressley, 1987).

Metacognition refers to higher order thinking which involves active control over the cognitive process engaged in learning. Activities such as planning how to approach a completion of a task are metacognitive in nature. Because metacognition plays a critical role in successful learning, it is important to study metacognitive activity and development to determine how students can be taught to better apply their cognitive resources through metacognitive control.

The term "meta-cognition" is most often associated with Flavell, (1979). According to Flavell (1979) Metacognitive consists of both meta-cognitive knowledge refers to acquired knowledge about cognitive process, knowledge that can be used to control cognitive process. Flavell future dividing meta-cognitive knowledge in to three categories:

a: Knowledge of person variable

b: Task variable

c: Strategy variables.

2.2.1   Meta-cognitive Knowledge

According to Bark (1990 meta-cognitive knowledge expends in three ways. Children become increasingly conscious of metacognitive capacities, of strategies of processing information and of task variables that facilitates performance. For Stanorck (2001) Metacognitive knowledge is about knowledge Cognition, mind and its working. Metacognitive knowledge includes insights such as the people including myself have limits to the amount of information they can process. It is not possible to deal all of information that comes our way. If we worry too much about this we will feel the stress of information overload. He further described metacognitive knowledge can benefit student learning. If students (especially young one) are deficient in metacognitive knowledge, this knowledge can possibly be thought to them. Several researchers have developed school programmed to improve metacognition knowledge. For example, you work in the quiet library rather than at home where there are many distractions. Knowledge of task variables includes knowledge about the nature of the task as well as the type of processing demands that it will place upon the individual For example, you may be aware that it will take more time for you to read and comprehend a science text than it would for you to read and comprehend a novel. Scantrock (2001).

2.2.2   Types of Meta-cognitive Knowledge

In Flavell's (1979) classic article on meta-cognition, he suggested that metacognition included knowledge of Strategy, task, and person. We represented this general framework in our categories by including students knowledge of general strategies for learning and thinking and their knowledge of cognitive tasks as well as when and why to use these different strategies. Finally, we include knowledge about self (the person variable) in relation to both cognitive and motivational components of performance.

2.2.2.1   Strategic Knowledge

Strategic knowledge as knowledge of general strategies for learning, thinking, and problem solving. These strategies are across all or most academic disciplines or subject matter domains in contrast to more Specific strategies from the disciplines or domains. Consequently, these Strategies can be used across a large number of different tasks and domains, rather than being most useful for one particular type of task in one specific subject area (e.g. solving a quadratic equation in mathematics applying Ohm's law in science. Strategic knowledge includes knowledge of the various strategies students might use to memorize material, to extract meaning from text, and to comprehend what they hear in classrooms or what they read in books and other course materials. Although there are a large number of different learning strategies, they can be grouped into three general categories: rehearsal, elaboration, and organizational.

Rehearsal strategies refer to the strategy of repeating words or terms to be remembered over and over to oneself, generally not the most effective strategy for learning more complex cognitive processes. In contrast, elaboration strategies include various mnemonics for memory tasks, as well strategies such as summarizing, paraphrasing, and selecting main ideas from texts. These elaboration strategies results in deeper processing of the material to be learned and result in better comprehension and learning than do rehearsal strategies. Finally, organizational strategies include various forms of outlining, concept mapping, and note taking, where the student makes connections between content elements. Like elaboration strategies, these organizational strategies usually result in better comprehension and learning than rehearsal strategies.

In addition to these general learning strategies, students can have knowledge of various metacognitive strategies that will be useful to them in planning, monitoring, and regulating their learning and thinking. These strategies include ways individuals plan their cognition (e.g. set goals) monitor their cognition (e.g. ask themselves questions as they read a piece of text; check their answer to a math problem) and regulates their cognition (e.g. re read something they don't understand; go back and 'repair' their calculating mistakes in a math problem). Again, I this category student's knowledge of these various strategies, not their actual use.

Finally, there are a number of general strategies for problem solving and thinking. These strategies represent the various heuristics. Individuals can use to solve problems, particularly ill-defined problems where there is no definitive algorithmic solution. In the problem-solving area they can include the knowledge of means-ends analysis as well as knowledge of working backward from the desired goal state. In terms of thinking, there are a number of general strategies for deductive and inductive thinking, such as evaluating the validity of different logical statements, avoiding circularity in arguments, making appropriate inferences from different sources of data, and drawing on appropriate samples to make inferences.

2.2.2.2 Metacognitive Knowledge About Problem-Solving Methods

Baker & Brown (1982) says that the effective application of Problem-solving method requires the knowledge of what task is relevant, what at the abilities involved are and how much effort is needed. However, as yet too little is known about these metacognitive representations this was aimed at describing beliefs about problem-Solving methods and assessing whether they vary according to the kind of method arid of problem and are modified by psychological courses attended. SAMPLE: Forty-six Italian undergraduates in psychology and 37 in non-psychological disciplines. METHODS: Participants had to rate how frequently each of five problem-solving methods (free production, analogy, step-by-step analysis, visualization and combining) is employed and how effective and easy each one is to apply. Rating were requested for interpersonal, practical and study problems. Participants were also asked to identify which abilities they thought would be involved in each method.

According to student's ratings, the most frequently used problem-solving method was analogy which was also considered the easiest method to apply, whereas step by step analysis and combining were considered the most difficult. Problem-solving techniques were perceived as being relevant above all for practical problems, whereas they were conceived as less suitable for interpersonal problems. F or study problems the most relevant strategy was step by step analysis. Students were aware of the abilities relevant to each problem-solving method.

Undergraduates both in psychology and non –psychological disciplines can identify some critical features in the methods used to solve Problems, even though some misconceptions emerged. Since metacognition plays an effective role in problem solving, trainers should take into account trainees' folk representations of problem-solving strategies.

14

2.3   General Metacognition

The concept of metacognition has been used to refer to variety of processes Brown (1978). It is defined knowledge or cognition that takes as its object or regulates any aspect of any cognitive endeavor. Brown (1978) distinguished between two dimensions of metacognition, namely knowledge about cognition and regulation of it. He suggested that knowledge about cognition can be "Stable, stable but fallible, or late developing", remaining relatively consistent within individuals. On the other hand, regulation of cognition, according to Brown (1978) can be "relatively unstable, rarely stable and age independent", changing rapidly from situation to situation. Brown's distinction suggests that the self regulation of cognition is more complex than age dependent; one may show self regulatory behavior in one situation but not in other, and a child may show self regulatory behavior where an adult does not. Regulation may also be effected by patterns of arousal (anxiety, fear, interest) and self concept (self-esteem, self-efficacy).

Rarely stable refers to the general inaccessibility of regulatory processes consciousness. Brown states that "conscious access to routines available to the system is highest form of mature human intelligence", which suggests that highly developed/metacognitive skill or ability to bring automated skills into consciousness, is characteristic of mature, developed humane intelligence (Pinard, 1986).

Pinard (1991) extend Flavell's definition of metacognitive by distinguishing between factual and strategic Meta knowledge. For Pinard, factual Meta knowledge overcome the three variables proposed by Flavell but enlarges its scope. According to Pinard, knowledge of Metacognition consists of

(1)   Objectives variable which relates to the motivational attitudes that we maintain towards our own learning
(2)   Task variables which he suggested had to be enlarged to include problem situations that individuals confront in their everyday lives.

15

(3)   Person variable, he suggests, it also needs to be enlarged to
        include cognitive –affective components such as motivational
        style, attribution style, self-efficacy and the internal dialogue that
        one engages in.

Pinard's strategic meta knowledge, however maintains a similar distinction
between cognitive and metacognitive strategies to the one initially proposed by
Flavell where cognitive strategies, or production strategies as suggested by
Pinard, refers to the repertoire of executive strategies that we have at our
disposal for producing a desired result whereas metacognitive strategies, or self-
regulatory strategies, refers to higher order strategies which serve to supervise
and regulate these and other strategies.

2.3.1   Metacognition Awareness

Baker (1989) defines knowledge ands strategies in isolation are not
sufficient for self-regulation. Students must understand the strengths and
limitations of their knowledge and strategies in order to be able to use them
efficiency. Educational psychologists' refer to this capability as metacognition, or
explicit knowledge of one's own

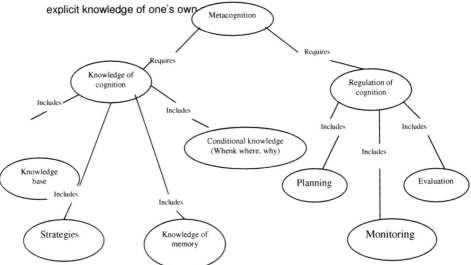

2.4   Regulation of Metacognition Activity

Pinard (1991) argue that metacognitive activity could be reduced exclusively to the simple enactment metacognitive knowledge, this is not the case. Rather, this activity remains subjected to certain pertinent factors which act as moderators of metacognitive activity and may include; attention, motivation, and the selection of goal congruent knowledge to be activated at the appropriate time in order to accommodate the current situations that present itself. Pinard (1991) suggests that self regulation is the key to unifying integrating the processes at work in metacognitive activity, since it functions essentially to coordinate the intervention of all the strategic and factual knowledge components.

Crowly, Shrager and Siegler (1997) demonstrated and studied the relationship between automation of cognitive processes and the emergences of metacgnitive thinking. Their results showed that Kindergarten children were most likely to think "meta-cognitively" When a lower level cognitive skill became automated. Crowley and colleagues suggested that strategies become "Associative Mechanism", which Operate without conscious effort and allow children to devote more mental processing space instead to learning. Gay (1999)

Veenman, Elshout and Meijer (1997) looked at task and domain variables in addressing generality verses domain-specificity of metacognitive skills in novices. They adopted what they called a "working model" approach. Individuals' working methods (metacognitive skills) can vary in quality. Expertise is the height of quality, with optimized knowledge and automat city, and a developed ability to do something of Self-regulatory skills in the domain of expertise.

Such quality is the result of repeated practice accumulation of related knowledge and general level of intelligence. Veenmen and colleagues used thinking allowed in problem solving simulations and coded them for orientation activities, systematic orderliness, accuracy, evaluation and elaborative activities together defining a working method.

17

2.5   Metacognition Intelligence & Adoptive Behavior

Strenberg (1989) says that "Theory of Human Intelligence includes what he calls metacomponents, or those features of intelligence that allows individuals to manage their cognitive resources." Stenberg model also consists of performance (encoding, decoding, mapping, application, and justification) knowledge acquisition components (selective encoding, selective combination, and selective comparison).

Those components represent automated cognitive and selective processes used in learning, respectively. Sternbeg consider met components to be a key feature of intelligence. Skills such as identifying the nature of a problem, planning, and monitoring, identified in the Triarchic model, are consistent with those characteristics associated with metacognition suggested by Flavell (1984).

The emphasis placed on metacomponents in Sternberg's theory, is on their association with adoptive behavior. These adaptive behaviors are considered to be functional strategies, or those that act on performance and knowledge acquisition components. Adaptive behavior goes beyond the knowledge and a cognitive ability measured by current intelligence tests, and represents the ability to use these aptitudes to adapt to, select, or shape one's environment.

The relationship between metacognitive knowledge and behavior, and learning disabilities remains. While some suggests that both general others suggests it is domain specific. A review of literature Suggests that both general and specific metacognitive abilities exist, A wide range of factors affects their development and functioning. For those with a reading disability, metacognitve defects appear to be specific reading tasks for those of higher intelligence, and generalized for that follower intelligence. Thinking or processing capacity may play a vital role in metacognitive behavior. When reading, insufficiently automated phonological skills results in more processing space required to decode print, thus using up processing space that could be devoted to higher level learning skills such as comprehension, critical, thinking and creativity. Such assumptions suggest that a good way to remedy this strain on processing space for those with a reading disability would be to have their reading done for them, the releasing them from the need to phonologically process print.

2.6.   Automation of Cognitive and Metacognitive Processes

Cravley (1997) and associates have demonstrated the relationship, between automation of cognitive processes and the emergence of metacognitive thinking. They found that kindergarten children were most likely to think "metacognitive" when a lower level cognitive skill became automated. They suggest that strategies become "Associative Mechanisms", which operate without conscious effort, allow children to devote more mental processing space to the metacognitive and curative aspects of learning.

Cravley (1997) further described that strategy eventually generalize by forming "goal sketches", which is the result of metacognitive mechanisms destroy from conscious access over time. Goal

Sketches are generalized strategies not particular to any task, but useful lacrosse many and used automatically based on recognition of general task characteristics. Such as retracing one's step to a lost item. Another such strategy could be attending to errors. If the initial letter to sound mapping in early readers does not become fully automated, it is possible this may result in reduced metacognitive activity in reading tasks where phonological ability is tested. Thus, metacomprehension, metamemory, and metalinguistic abilities may be hindered because extra processing space is requiring to process phonological input.

He further postulates that children with the automation of lower level basic skills may be delay or deficient, thus emergence of goal sketches or automated generalized strategies, may also be delayed or deficient. This is consistent with findings that suggest internalization of private speech is delayed in children with a reading disability insufficiently automated phonological processes delay suppression of externalized private speech. It is not clear whether the inability to develop or initiate generalized strategies is a domain general phenomenon or specific to domain of the disability. It may be that such skills are developed but

19

are not accessible when the domain of the disability is being challenged. That is, when a child with a reading disability is reading, the strain on processing space prevents the emergence of metacognitive behaviors, while on tasks that do not require reading metacognitive behaviors can emerge.

2.7.   Metacognitive Development

A few century before as the century draws to a close cognitive regulation as secure a center stage role for the study of cognition I a broad array of both laboratory and 'situated" context although it ultimately may prove as consequential, is an increasingly important role occupied by the second order construct of metacognition cognition about cognition. Most account of metacognition involves conscious awareness of mental activity, psychologist's study of metacogitive phenomena stand to inform and constrain theories of consciousness. Nelson (1996)

Nelson (1996) describe that edition educators increasingly see it as important for students to "take charge of their own learning" rather than accept the passive role of being recipient of what others have to till them. In each of these cases, students "Meta cognitive awareness and management of their own cognitive process is implicated. If educators are to realize such goals, their need psychological knowledge of metacognitive process, how they develop, and how they can be fostered.

2.7.1   Forms of Meta-Knowing

With developmental psychology, the rotes of current interest in metacognitive phenomena are both arrow and broad. The earliest work dealt almost exclusively with awareness and monitoring of memory strategies. Brown (1997), Metacognition "thinking about thinking" in a wide range of both traditional a modern theory of cognitive development. (Metacognition is not a zero-one phenomenon that emerges at some single, identifiable point in development). Even very young children have Meta-cognitive competencies. Brown (1997) yet thinking of adult's reveals serious weaknesses in metacognitive awareness and control. Kuhn (1991) Kuhn (1991) further contended that this conception of a gradually developing metacognitive competence offers a unifying perspective for connecting variety of developmental phenomena that may not seem closely linked on surface, but all have to do with the emergence and development and of second order cognation. In particularly there are un-connected bodies of work that wish to being together. First; those addressing meta-knowing about knowing processors versus knowing products. Second; investigation of the meta-knowing competencies of Young children verses older individuals. Another distinction in forms of meta-knowing is one between awareness of cognition and understanding of its content. In addition to awareness and understanding, Third; form consists of the attempt to influence one's cognition through process of monitoring resources allocation of other form of management Khan (1991).

2.7.2   Developmental origins of Meta-Knowing

As Kazdin (2000) says that children participate in social culture transforms their experience in a powerful ways. Still recognizing the power of culture is not sufficient to explain the process by which the child constructs meaning through participation in it. Analysis must include the meaning making activity of the participants in this collective experience. The capacity of Meta representation of meaning develop early in life certainly by the two years as reflected by such traditional indicators as pretend play and 'imitation by three age children are able to verbalized their awareness that the world includes not only material but also non material one's such as desires, intentions, thoughts, an ideas that are the product of human mental life. (Flavell & Miller.1997). They are able to distinguish mental entitles form physical one's. In everyday conversation children by age three make reference to their own knowledge states using verbs such as think and know and may even express awareness of absence of knowledge.

2.8   Developing Students Metacognitive Knowledge and Strategies

Metacognition in learning and tutoring describes ways to help students develop and apply metacognitive knowledge and strategies. A strategy is defined as a conscious, deliberate use of a specific method, where a skill is defined as a refined strategy which is used selective, automatically and unconsciously as needed. From an information processing perspective, metacognitive, executive control processes, which guide the flow of information through the mind and regulate cognition, explain why some students learn and remember more than others Wool folk (1980). High achieving students have been found to possess more metacognitive awareness and engage in more self-regulatory behavior than low achieving students. Uses of metacognitive knowledge and strategies, and domain-specific knowledge have been important roles in thinking and problem solving.

Sternberg's diarchic theory of intelligence suggests that high-achieving students are more metacognitve than low-achieving students. Characterizes the metacognitive processes of self-regulated learners in terms of planning, setting goals, organizing, self-monitoring and self-evaluating at various times during the learning process. Zimmerman (1995) points out that it is not enough for students to have metacognitive knowledge they also must self-regulate its use when confronted with stress, competing attractions and fatigue. Context-dependent motivational issues, such as effort, self-efficacy, persistence and task choice are also important determinants of self-regulation. Metacognition is necessary, but not sufficient, for academic success. The further indicates that the importance of attention higher level thinking (including problem solving, metacognition, and critical thinking) and affect (including motivation, self-concept, and affective self-regulation and attributions) in addition to the traditional focus on content and basic skills. Leaning s best when it is active, meaningful, retained over time, and transfers to a variety of contexts.

A vitally important but often neglected aspect of learning is that often students have the re use knowledge and skills for performing complex tasks but do not use them; i.e., the skills remain. Some times students are not motivated or confident to apply them, and sometimes students simply do not recognize that the situation calls for use of particular knowledge and skills. That is, students may have declarative and procedural knowledge, but not the contextual or conditional knowledge needed for application and transfer. Garner's (1990) theory of Settings that the nature of strategic activity often varies with the context. She notes that children and adults often fail to use the strategies at their disposal because minimal transfer, attributions and classroom goals do not support strategy use, the knowledge base is not adequately developed, and learners tend to use primitive routines and show poor cognitive monitoring. According to Garner (1990) theory of settings there are at least six contextual factors that affect strategy use. These factors include strategies being too tightly linked to particular situations, lack of knowledge about the relationship between strategy use and task demands, and classroom settings that do not value the effortful application of strategies. Hartman (1993).

Although over the past two decades research has documented the important role of metacognition in learning, many students are of the concept of metacognition might be reflect on their thinking and learning strategies and attitudes and how they might be improved. Knowing about your own thinking about your own thinking-metacognitvtion includes thinking about your own thinking processes and the products of your thinking. Two fundamental aspects of metacognition are executive management strategies for planning, monitoring, and revising one's thinking processes and products, and strategic knowledge about what information and strategies/skills one has (declarative), when and why to use them (contextual/conditional), and how to use them (procedural). Metacognition is domain general, applying across subjects and situations; and some is domain-specific, applying selectively to particular subjects and situations. The development of metacognition beings around five to seven years of age and is enhanced during and through schooling Flavell (1985).

Cognitive (worker) skills perform the intellectual work decided on by the metacognitive bosses. Examples of cognitive skills include encoding (registering information, inferring, comparing, and analyzing. Metacognition refers to "thinking about thinking", such as deciding how to approach a task. Metacognitive (boss) skills involve executive management processes such as planning, monitoring and evaluating. Although cognitive skills are important Sternberg (1986) argue that teaching needs to emphasize metacognitive skills because:

1.   Teaching specific strategies, such as the order in which to perform a particular task, will not give students the skills they need in the long run. Students must learn general principles such as planning, and   how to apply them over a wide variety of tasks and domains.

2.   Both the long-term benefits of training in cognitive skills and the ability to apply cognitive skills to new tasks appear to depend, at least in pert, on training at the metacognitive level as well as at the cognitive performance.

3.   Generally students have a history of blindly following instructions. They have not acquired the habit of questioning themselves to lead to effective to lead to effective performance on intellectual tasks.

4   Students with the greatest metacognitive skill deficiencies seem to have no idea what they are doing when performing a task.

5.   Students have metacognitive performance problem of; (a) determining the difficulty of a task 9b) monitoring their comprehension effectively, i.e. they don't recognize when they don't fully understand something (e.g. task directions, information in textbook) (c) planning ahead (e.g. what they need to do and how long each part should take 0 (d0 monitoring the success of their performance or determining when they have studied enough to master the material to be learned (e) using all relevant information (f) using a systematic step- by-step approach; & jumping to conclusions; and using inadequate or incorrect representations. Metacognitive skills and knowledge, as important as they are not often taught in most areas of curriculum.

2.9   Metacognitive Reading Strategies

Alexander's (1995) metacognition is affected by the level of One's knowledge in a particular domain. Novice learners are likely to engage in metacognitve activities less often and less successfully than learners with more subject area knowledge, who are at the competence stage of learning in a domain. Baker (1989) reviewed some recent studies with adult readers. She found that in general, good readers, who are good students, appear to have more awareness and control over their own cognitive activities while reading than the poor readers, in her characterization of the "expert reader", Baker noted that research on metacognitive strategies shows that they interact with domain specific knowledge. For example, experts and novices in specific domains differ in how they budget and regulate their reading time. Domain-knowledge sometimes includes metacognitive knowledge of the relative effectiveness of various strategies. Studies comparing good and poor readers identify a variety of metacognitive skills that enhance reading comprehension. According to Brown (1980) and others, good readers regularly plan, attend to task demands, predict, use strategies to increase their comprehension and meet task requirements, check, monitor, reality test, control and coordinate their learning. Four effective reading comprehension strategies found by Jones, Amiran and Katims (1985) were; organizational, Contextual and reflective thinking and imagery strategies. Long and Long (1987) reported that good comprehend in college are more mentally active while reading than are poor comprehenders. Good comprehenders engage in mental interactions with the text through visualizing, self-questioning, and inferring. Although poor comprehenders engage in some metacognitive activities, such as skimming, rereading and pointing to key words, they perform behaviors similar to those of good comprehenders, but without mentally activating operations needed for understanding.

He further explains in addition to this specific, conditional or contextual information about strategy use, individuals may need to know other information about using the strategies. What good is it to tell a subject when to form a mental image if the subject doesn't know exactly what is meant by a mental image? The strategic knowledge base must include extensively declarative information, facts about the world in general and the particular domain, like the imagery strategy and its application to reading. Declarative knowledge interacts with strategy execution; it is often needed to implement the appropriately identified strategy.

Finally, it may be important for a person being instructed to know step-by-step procedures for how to create one and regulate its use. Self-regulation includes the ability to monitor and evaluate strategy use.

Metacognitive reading skills include: skimming, activating relevant Prior knowledge, constructing mental images, predicting, self-questioning, and comprehension monitoring, summarizing and connecting new material with prior knowledge. Students cannot be expected to be competent with these skills because they are rarely taught and not everyone develops them independently. They need to explicitly and continually addressed, practiced, polished and internalized. Improvements in these skills can lead to dramatic improvements in academic achievement. Students who are aware and in control of their metacognitive reading behaviors are at a distinct advantage because many of them involve monitoring one's comprehension, taking steps to clarify difficulties and restoring the comprehension process when it has broken down. Effective instruction in metacognitive reading skills requires that teachers explain the skills or strategies, model them for students, give examples, explain when, why, and how to use them, emphasize the value of flexibility in selecting specific skills to fit the particular context, provide guided

Practice on a range of texts, and give corrective feedback. Palinsar and Brown's (11984) reciprocal teaching procedure is specifically designed to develop four metacognitive skills: questioning, clarifying, summarizing and predicting. Through reciprocal teaching, eventually students are able to apply these metacognitive reading strategies on their own as self-regulating readers. Ecles (1998).

Research on college reading and study skills notes that there is a trend across studies showing that students perception of their own control tend to affect their time management, use of reading strategies, and test taking; previous research on control theory suggests that unless students perceive that they have some control over and can influence their environment, their capacity to learn from instruction is limited. Maxwell (1993) Garner argues that explanations about reading comprehension strategies should include: why the strategy should be learned; what the strategy is, how to use it, when and where to use the strategy and how to evaluate strategy use. Elementary school teachers do little direct instruction in how to comprehend text (Durkin, 1981).

2.10 Self-Regulating and Metacognition

According to (Laura, 1999) self-regulation is the second aspect of Metacognition. Self-regulation is the process of continuously monitoring progress towards a goal checking outcomes and redirecting and unsuccessful efforts. According to Schunk (1999) researcher to find that high achieving student often engage in self-regulatory activity such as setting specific learning goals self monitoring their learning and systematically evaluating their progress toward a goal.

For Pint rich goal setting, planning and self-regulation are important dimensions and achievements. Goal setting and planning often work in concert when individuals set goals they need to plan how to reach these goals. Goals help individuals to reach their dream increase their Self-displine and maintain interest. According to Wigfield (1997) their has been little research on how children goals develop. Performance goals likely are establish in elementary schools years and become increasingly common in the adolescent as well as adult set goals and then develop plans to reach the goals. Especially young children youth should be encouraged to engage in goal setting and planning activities. Parents and teachers who encourage children to become self-regulatory learners. Conway the message that children are responsible for their own behavior and that achievement requires active and delegated effort.

2.10.1 Occurrence of Self-Regulation

According to Bandura (1996) self-regulation involves monitoring or observing one own behavior and using various techniques for regulation behavior such as self-reinforcement, self-punishment. Self-reinforcement is a process whereby individuals improve and maintain their own behavior by giving them selves rewards over which they have control whenever they attain certain self imposed standards of performance since both negative as well as positive self reaction is possible. From Bandura's perspective self-regulated incentives increase performance mainly through their motivational function. That is by making Self-gratification or tangible reward conditional upon realizing certain accomplishment. Individuals motivate themselves to expand the effort needed to attain the desire performance. The individuals the level of self-induce motivation aroused by this mean usually varies according to the type and value of the incentives and the nature of the performance standards.

He further says there are three components process involved in the self-regulation of behavior by self produced consequences, self observation judgment and self response process. He further says the individuals previous behaviors also provide a standard against which the adequacy of on going performance may be judged. Baundra suggest that fast performance influence self-appraisal principally through its impact on goal setting. "After a given level of performance is attained it is no longer challenging and new self-satisfaction or sort through progressive improvements". Students after tended to raise their performance standards. Success and to lower them too more realistic levels after repeated failure.

2.10.2   Self-regulatory Learning

According to Winne & Perry as cited in Smith (2000). Self-regulatory learning consists of the self-generation and self monitoring of thoughts, feeling, and behavior to reach a goal. These goals might be academic or they might be social, emotional.

According to Zimmerman as cited in Bark (1999). Describe the characteristic of self-regulated learners. Set goals for extending their knowledge and sustaining their motivation. Are aware of their emotional make up and have strategies for managing their emotions. Periodically monitor tiers progress toward a goal, Fine tune or revise their strategies bases on the progress they are making. Evaluate obstacles that arise and make the necessary adoption.

According to Presley's cited in Bernard (1994) to continue learning independently throughout life, you must be self-evaluated learners; self-regulated learners have the skills and the ill to learn. These factors influences skill and will Knowledge Motivation Volition

Knowledge

According to Alexander as cited in Bernard (1994) self-regulated learners, students need knowledge about themselves, subject, and the task strategies for learners and the content in which they will apply there learning. "Expert" students know about themselves and how they learn best. For example they know their proffered learning themselves, what is easy and what is hard for them, how to copy with the hard parts, what that interest and talent are. And how to use there strange. These experts also known quite a but about the subject being studied and the more they know, the easier it is to learn more. They probably understand that different learning tasks require different approaches on their parts. A simple memory task, for example might require a mnemonic strategy. Where a complex comprehension task might be approached by means of concept maps of the key ideas. Also these self-regulate learners know that learning often is difficult and knowledge is seldom absolute there usually are different ways of looking at problems as well as different solutions.

According to Wang & Palincsar as cited in Bernard (1994) these experts students mot only know what back task-require, and the can also apply the strategy needed. They can skim or read carefully. They can mnemonics or recognize the material. As they become more knowledge able in a field, they many of those strategies automatically, finally, expert learners think about the context where they will apply their knowledge when and where they will use their learning. So they can set Motivating goals and connect present work to future accomplishment. In short they have mastered a large, flexible repertoire of learning strategies and tactics.

Motivation

According to Corno as cited in Bernard (1994) says, self regulated learners are motivated to learn. They find many tasks in school interesting they value learning, net just performing well in the eyes of others. But even if they are not intrinsically motivated by a particular task, they are studying, so their actions and choices are self-determined and not control by others. However knowledge and motivations are not always enough. Self-regulated learners also need volitions or self-discipline.

Volition

According to Ormrod, (1998) volition is an old-fashioned word for will power. Self-regulated learners know how to protect themselves from distractions where to study, for example so they are not interrupted they know how to cope when they feel anxious, drowsy, or lazy. And they know what to do when tempted to stop working.

Ormrod (1998) further says, obviously, not all the students will be self-regulated learners. Infact some psychologists suggests that you think this capacity as individual difference characteristics. Some students are much better than others. So there are three factors which influence the skill and will of self regulated learners.

According to Wade (1998) self-regulation is a strong predicator of academic success. Students who do well in school know when they posses a skill and when they do not. If they run up against obstacles, such as poor study condition, a confusing text passage or an unclear class lecture, they take steps to organized learning environment review the material or seek other sources of support.

Wode (1998) further indicates most high achieving students; high students are self-regulatory learners. For example, compared with low achieving students, high students set more specific learning goals, use more strategies to learn, self-monitor their learning more and more systematically evaluate their progress toward a goal.

According to Barry as cited in Berk (1999) developed of a model of turning low self-regulatory students into students who engaged in these multi step strategies;

    i.   Self-evaluation and monitoring ,

    ii.   Goal setting and strategies planning.

    iii.   Putting plan into action and monitoring it

    iv.   Monitoring outcomes and refining strategies. at who engaged in these multi step strategies"rk (1999) developed of a model of turning low self-regulatory students into s

A MODEL OF SELF- REGULARTORY LEARNING

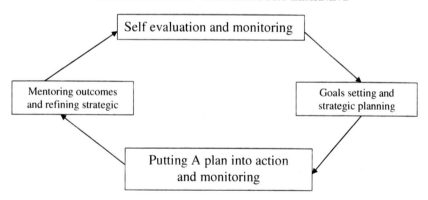

Monitoring outcomes and Refining Strategies, Self-Evaluation and Monitoring putting a plan into action and monitoring it, Goal setting and strategic planning.

A model of self-regulatory learning. They describe a seventh grade student who is doing poorly in history and apply their self-regulatory model) to her situation. In grade one she self-evaluates by keeping a detailed record of them. The teacher gives her some comprehension of difficult reading materials. In grade two the student sets a goal, in this case of improving reading comprehension, and plans how to achieve the goals. The teacher assists her in breaking down the goal into components parts, such as locating for main ideas and setting specific goals understanding a series of paragraph in her textbook.

The teacher also provide the student initially on the first sentences of each paragraph and then scanning the others as a means of identifying main ideas. Another comprehension if it is available. In their grade the students' puts the plan into action ad being to monitor her progress. Initially they might need help from the teacher or tutor in

identifying main ideas in the reading. This feedback can help her monitor her reading comprehension more effectively on her own. In fourth grade students monitor her improvement in reading comprehension by evaluating whether it has had any impact on her learning outcomes. Most importantly; has her importance in reading comprehension lead to better performance on history test. So through the performance of self-regulation students can regulated their learning Bert (1999).

2.11   Self-Regulatory System and Plans

According to Crozier (19970 many people regulated their behavior by rewarding or not rewarding for certain action some students decide that they will treat themselves to a movie or a chocolate ice cream soda after finish each term paper. If they stick to these plans, they have good incentives to get their work doe. Giving themselves rewards for doing the work likely to establish a behavior pattern that matches persona standards and lead to man valued outcomes in the long run. And self-punishment to arranging for an aversive consequence for failing to achieve a goal such as depriving yourself of something you enjoy or making yourself to an unpleasant task. Depending on the kind of behavior you want to change, various combinations of self-reinforcement and self-punishment etc may be used.

2.12   Self-Regulation of Thinking and Learning

The term self-regulated learning (SRL) became popular in the 1980's because it emphasized the emerging autonomy and responsibility of students to take charge of their own learning. As a general term, it subsumed research on cognitive strategies, metacognition, and motivation in one coherent construct that emphasized the interplay among these forces. It was regarded as a valuable term because it emphasized how the "self" was the agent in establishing learning goals and tactics and how each individual's perceptions of the self and task influenced the quality of learning that ensured. In the past ten years, a great deal of research has focused on a constructivist perspective on SRL (Paris & Byrnes, 1989), on social foundations of SRL on developmental changes in SRL, and on instructional tactics for promoting SRL. The integrative nature of SRL stimulated researchers to study broader and more contextualized issues of teaching and learning while also showing the value of SRL as an educational objective at all grade levels. Interested readers can trace the history and various theoretical orientations to SRL. What is important for teacher educators is that SRL can help describe the ways that people approach problems, apply strategies, monitor their performance, and interpret the outcomes of their efforts. In this brief overview, we focus on three central characteristics of SRL; awareness of thinking, use of strategies, and sustained motivation. Schunk Zimmerman 91989)

2.12.1   Awareness of Thinking

Part of becoming self-regulated involves awareness of effective thinking and analysis of one's own thinking habits. This is metacognition, or thinking about thinking, that Flavell (1978) and Brown (1978) first described.

They showed that children from 5-16 years of age become increasingly aware of their own personal knowledge states, the characteristics of tasks that influence learning, and their own strategies for monitoring learning. Paris and Winograd (1990) summarized these aspects of metacognition as children's developing competencies for self-appraisal and self-management and discussed how these aspects of knowledge can help direct student's effort as they learn. We tried to emphasize that the educational goal was not simply to make children think about their own thinking but, instead to use metacognitive knowledge to guide the plans they make, the strategies they select, and the interpretations of their performance so that awareness leads to effective problem-solving. Our approach is consistent with Bandura (19860 who emphasized that self-regulation involves three interrelated processes; self-observation, self-evaluation, and self-reaction. Understanding these processes and using them deliberately is the metacognitive part of SRL.

2.12.2   Use of Strategies

Flavell (1978) further explain that part of SRL involves a Person's growing repertoire of strategies for learning, studying, controlling emotions, pursuing goals, and so forth. However, we want to emphasize that our concern is with "being strategic" rather than "having' a strategy. It is one thing to know what a strategy is and quite a different thing to be inclined to use, to modify it as task conditions change, and to

be able to discuss it and teach it. There are three important metacognitive aspects of strategies, often referred to as declarative knowledge (what the strategy is), procedural knowledge (how the strategy operates), and conditional knowledge (when and why a strategy should be applied)

Knowing these characteristics of strategies can help students to discriminate productive from counterproductive tactics and then to apply appropriate strategies. When students are strategic, they consider options before choosing tactics to solve problems and then they invest effort in using the strategy. These choices embody SRL because they are the result of cognitive analysis of alternative routes to problem solving.

2.12.3 Sustained Motivation

The third aspect of SRL is motivation because learning requires effort and choices. Kuhn argued that ordinary learning fuses skill and will together in self-directed actions. SRL involves motivational decisions about the goal of an activity, the perceived difficulty and value of the task, the self-perceptions of the learner's ability to accomplish the task, and the potential benefit of success or liability of failure. Awareness and reflection can lead to a variety of actions depending on the motivation of the person. Researchers and educators have characterized SRL as a positive set of attitudes, strategies, and motivations for enhancing thoughtful engagement with tasks but students can also be self-directed to avoid learning or to minimize challenges. When students act to avoid failure instead of pursue success, attribute their performance to external or uncontrollable forces, use self-handicapping strategies, or set inappropriate goals, they are undermining their own learning. These behaviors are self-regulated but may also be counterproductive motivational responses to learning that can be overcome with better understanding of SRL. In our view, teachers need to understand student's motivation in order to understand how they learn, what tasks they choose, and why they may display persistence and effort or, conversely, avoidance and apathy. Self-regulation thus implies "personalized cognition and motivation" that examples behaviors that may or may not be consistent with the teacher's agenda for learning. Because teachers need to be diagnostic about their student's learning styles and orientations, it is helpful to analyze student's awareness, use of strategies, and their motivation Pasis (198. It is important to note that our view of self-regulated learning does not conflict with Borko and Putnam's view of Cognition as situated, social, and distributed. They argue, and we agree that to understand knowledge and learning, we must better understand the importance of contexts, social relationships, collaboration, and cooperation. Self-regulated learning does not mean that knowledge and learning exists solely in the mind of an individual. Rather, self-regulated learning recognizes that individuals have some control over their own learning, across contexts, across relationships, and across situations. We think that teachers who use a psychological leads to analyze students strategies, motivation, and attitudes gain deeper understand about students' behavior in the classroom which, in turn, allows them to design better instruction that can make learning more meaningful for them. Pasis (1983).

2.12   Self-Regulate in Math and Sciences

College math and sciences courses are never easy. Students can make steady incremental progress, however, if they follow the four-step plan outlined in this paper:

- Spend enough time (i.e. make the effort to learn and persist when
- learning is difficult)
- Accumulate an integrated knowledge base
- Develop a repertoire of strategies appropriate for the present course, and
- Believe they can succeed These four steps are illustrated in

36

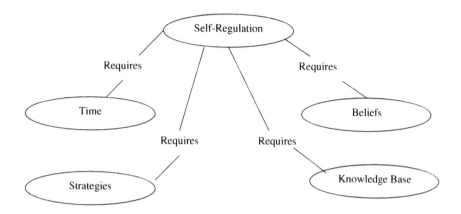

Using the four-step plan above helps students become self- regulated because it gives them an explicit plan for improving their success in math and science courses, and helps them understand the integral relationship between knowledge, strategies and motivation. Without self-regulatory skills, students are at great risk of dropping out or failing because they attribute their learning problems to lack of ability (Graham, 1991). Gradm (1991) further indicates that throughout we emphasize the important role of effort in learning. We also examine how to increase the effectiveness of effort via motivational factors and strategy use in college-level math and science courses. We first define these constructs, and then briefly review recent research from educational psychology that supports their inclusion in classrooms. We next provide suggestions for enhancing the motivational climate of classrooms and a six-step plan for improving strategy use. We emphasize the role of motivational beliefs and strategies for two reasons. One is that each plays a distinct and important role in learning. The other is that both are feasible to short-term classroom interventions meaning that you can have a measurable impact with in the duration of your courses.

2.14   The Role of Metacognition in Learning

In the last ten years of international discussions about mathematics education, it has increasingly been discussed to make reflection and metacognition a central component of mathematics teaching. We will analysis components of metacognition that are employed during understanding of mathematical concepts and procedures. We will develop a theoretical model and apply it to the analysis of teaching scenes. All scenes have in common that with in mutually shared discursive lesson culture pupils discuss the interplay of external and internal, mental representation, of the things being said and those being meant.

Metacognition defined as thinking about one's own thinking and its role in conceptual change and problem solving in learning. Educational research shows that promoting metacognition in the science classroom prompts students to refine their ideas about scientific concepts and improves their problem-solving success. Examples of how metacognition affects problem-solving success are presented, some instructional tools those have been employed to promote metacognition the introductory science planning and generating.

2.15   Measuring Metacognition

Measuring metacognitive processes has been difficult. Many of the instruments developed to measure have suffered critism about their validity. This section looks at some of these instruments, out lining pros and cons of cons of each, and goes on to suggest use of behavioral measures which eliminate many of the influences such as social desirability effects and limited conscious access to subconscious automated skills, both of which affect responses to questions about cognitive and metacognitive processes.

1)   The vast majority of reports, in which individuals recall what they were thinking while they were doing a task;

2   Concurrent verbal reports, in which they record their thinking while it is occurring,

3) Written reports, in which individuals record their thinking in response to standardized questions following a task; and

4) Self-estimates, in which individuals estimate their performance on a task prior to, or after completing it. Each of these methods suffers from validity problems. Retrospective interviews rely on often vague memories of one's thinking during problem solving. Concurrent reports interfere with cognitive processing in progress. Standardized written reports rely on memory and are limited by the standard questions they ask. As suggested by Brown.

5) Regulatory skills can be relatively unstable, rarely stat able, and age independent, suggesting here that self reports of behavior may at best reveal only a small portion of the cognitive and metacognitive activity that occurs during problem solving, and at worst reveal a fabricated account of these processes.

One of the most commonly used measures of metacognition has been the "Feeling of Knowing" judgment; after failing to answer a test item, individuals are asked to judge how well they think they would do in a multiple choice recognition test in which one of the alternatives was the correct answer. "Ease of learning" judgments (also called confidence judgments or self-estimates) are another measure of metacognition; individuals predict, given a test's requirements, how well they think they will perform on it. Similarly," Judgments of learning" have individuals predict how well they did on a test just completed. Predicted and actual performance is compared on each of these measures, of which the absence of a discrepancy is assumed to indicate access to knowledge about one's self and cognitive abilities. Studies to date find little or no relationship between these measures however, and results are not reliably similar across testing periods or content these measure however, and results are not reliably similar across testing periods or content areas.

Self-estimates fare better than verbal or written reports however, comparing predictions of performance to actual performance rather than relying on memory or intrusive questioning. Self-estimates still run the risk of social desirability effects interfering with the accuracy of the measure, which is respondents may tell the tester what he or she wants to hear whether it is what actually happened or not.

Despite their shortcomings, such measures are necessary until the time behavioral measures become more readily available to record the interaction between cognition, metacognition, knowledge, and ability, and can be recorded "online" through unobtrusive mechanical means. Observation of individuals while problem solving can reveal a variety of behaviors that indicate metacognitive activity Jeg, scratch a chin, raise an eyebrow. While observation can reduce social desirability and cognitive access issues, only a small portion of meta-cognitive behavior may be overtly displayed, and agreement as to what constitutes a metacognitive behavior can reduce the usefulness of observational data. Eye movement and response times can provide behavioral measures which are not as influenced by the factors just outlined that have affected the validity of verbal and self reports. Ideally both behavioral measures and verbal repots should be used, comparing what & person says they were doing at a particular point in a task with what their eyes and mind were doing at that time.

So in addition to self-reports, behavioral performance measures are needed in which individuals behaviors are recorded online as they complete a task. Online data can help corroborate self-reports and observational data, and provide valuable information about patterns of learning and the association between overt and covert metacognitive behaviors. Post-Failure Reflectivity and Pre-Failure Reflectivity are two such online measures that capture the behavior of attending to errors, by recording response times prior to and following successful and failed responses on an inference task. Attention to errors is assumed to be a metacognitive activity involving internal dialogue, analysis. Reflection, each involved in the evaluation of a mistake.

The typical test of reflectivity has individuals complete a series of computerized test items, receiving feedback after each item, either negative (following an error), or positive (following a correct response), then requesting the next item and repeating the process. The computer records accuracy and response and post-response times. It is assumed that those who spend more time after a failed response before requesting the next item, are attending to the error they have just made. In effect they are learning from their mistake, perhaps one of the most effective learning strategies. It is also assumed that those who spend more time before answering a question in correctively are anticipating an impending error, thus attempting to delay or avoid receiving negative feedback, reconsidering their answer, having the knowledge that they are going to answer incorrectly, and delaying receipt of negative feedback. These error-attending behaviors are metacognitive in nature.

CHAPTER 3

Summary

Purpose of this review based study was to explore the role of metacognition in enhancing learning. Metacognition play vital role in learning. It is important for improving student's learning. It develops higher order thinking in students. Metacognition is a process in which we improve the ideas that develop most effective thinking and awareness. Metacognition refers to awareness and understanding of various aspect of thought.

Self regulation is part of metacognition. Knowledge and strategies are not sufficient for self-regulation. Metacognition include metacognitive experience, things that happen to you that pertain to you knowledge or understanding of your own metacognitive process. Metacognition refers to one's knowledge concerning

41

one's own cognitive processes or anything related to them. We engage in meta-cognitive activities everyday. Metacognition refers to higher order thinking which involves active control over the cognitive process engaged in learning.

Self-regulation involves monitoring or observing one own behavior and using various techniques for regulation behavior such as self-reinforcement, self-punishment. Researchers and educators have characterized self regulatory learning as a positive set of attitudes, strategies, and motivations for enhancing thoughtful engagement with tasks but students can also be self-directed to avoid learning or to minimize challenges.

Metacognition plays a critical role in successful learning, it is important to study meta-cognitive activity and development to determine how students should be taught to better apply their cognitive resources through meta-cognitive control.

3.1 Findings

Metacognition has been shown to be significantly related to a variety of describable outcomes. Metacognition has been shown to act as a useful predictor of turnover (learning achievement) self-regulation is a part of metacognition.It is a sort of self monitor behavior. Well developed metacognition ability have well developed Self-regulation students can monitor their own learning progress. Metacognition generates higher order thinking.

3.2 Conclusion

Metacognition refer to knowledge of one's cognitive abilities. Metacognition consist of both metacognitive knowledge and metacognitive experiences or regulation.

1.   Metacognitive knowledge refers to acquired acknowledgement about cognitive processes, knowledge that can be used control cognitive processes metacognitive knowledge can three categories: knowledge of person variables, task variables and strategy variables. Metacognitive knowledge is knowledge about cognition, mind and its working. Strategic knowledge is knowledge of general strategies for learning, thinking, and problem solving; these strategies usually result in better comprehension and learning than rehearsal strategies.

2.   Students can have knowledge of various metacognitive strategies useful in planning, monitoring, and regulating learning and thinking. Knowledge of metacognition consist of: (a) Person variables or knowledge about one's self and other's thinking (b) Task variables or knowledge that different types of tasks exert different types of cognitive demands and (c) Strategy variable or knowledge about cognitive and metacognitive strategies for enhancing, learning and performance.

3.   Recent research highlights the importance of both metacognitive knowledge and metacognitive skills in learning. These methods of helping students acquire metacognitive knowledge and skills to improve their learning. That research on metacognition in learning and tutoring and describes ways to help students develop and apply metacognitive knowledge and strategies. Metacognitive knowledge and skills are needed for effective cognitive performance. Domain knowledge sometimes includes metacognitive knowledge of the relative effectives of various strategies.

4.   Self regulatory learning consists of the self-regulation and self- monitoring of thoughts, feeling, and behavior to reach a goal. Self- regulated learners also need self-discipline. Researches have found that most high achieving students are self-regulatory learners. Several teaching strategies have been identified as promoting self-regulated learning.

5.   Self-regulation involves three interrelated processes; self-observation, self-evaluation, and self-regulated learning does not all ages need to control their learning through productive motivational beliefs and use of cognitive learning strategies.

6.   Knowledge and strategies in isolation are not sufficient for self-regulation. Understanding self-regulation can help teachers make thinking public and visible control and self-regulatory processes are cognitive processes that learners use to monitor, control, and regulate their cognition and learning. Student's performance can be enhanced by developing metacognitive knowledge child's lower and with the passage of time it can be developed to higher level.

3.4   Recommendations

Metacognition plays critical role in successful learning. It has been found that
Metacognition is the most important for the improving performance of students learning. In reading and thinking process use students the metacognitive process and use get better results. It develops higher level thinking in students. To used metacognition about their subject.

Metacognition is a process in which we improve our mental approach about solution of any problem. Through metacognition we can know about our mental approach and its levels. Either our mental approach is appropriate to our statement or problems of or not. Relationships between our statement and views are same or not. It is only possible when our brain approach is sufficient and able to resume any problem.

Metacognition can use to enhance students learning and memory. Critical age of development of metacognition is to 7 to 8 year. Its strategies are useful for planning, monitoring and regulation of learning and thinking. Metacognitive skills are involved in management process such as planning, monitoring and evaluating. Metacognitive knowledge and skills are needed for effective cognitive performance.

Through different researches it has been found that students improve their performance, thinking and learning by using metacognitive strategies. I think that metacognition is related to awareness its mea that we are aware about our mind and can understand we I think and we known. Psychologist has described two types of metacognition.

1. Knowledge about cognition
2. Regulation of that knowledge

Metacognition is also beneficial in social, emotional and adoptive behavior. Self-regulation is the second part of metacognition. Self-regulation is the process of continuously monitoring of thoughts, feeling and behavior to reach a goal. Self regulation is most important for those students who have higher level ability. By using self-regulation, students increase their learning, make it interesting, set their goals and try to achieve them.

Parents and teachers can develop children's self regulatory skills by promoting out, special demands of test by encouraging the use of strategies and emphasizing the value of self correction.

To explore better results, students, use self reinforcement process and this is a process where by individuals improve and maintain their own behavior by giving themselves reward over which they have control whenever they attain certain self-imposed standards of performance since both negative as well as positive self reactions are possible. Students who set their goals for extending knowledge and sustaining motivation are aware of their motivational makeup and have strategies for managing them.

I think that metacognition at initial level is not high. But when time passed metacognition improves and fulfill every crition. Same as when children are at primary level their mental level are at initial stage and they can not learn everything around their environment and same as in their studies. But when time passes and children moves toward their graduate level their mental ability improve and also improve their metacognition and mental level.

Recommendations

- Metacognition is helpful in improving students learn ability that is why teacher must use this techniques.
- Metacognition can be used in curriculum development.
- In teaching specific strategies such as the order in which to perform a particular their will not give students the skills they need in the long run. Students must learn techniques, e.g. planning, monitoring etc and these can be learnt through metacognition.
- It may be used to improve cognition performance.
- Metacognition should necessarily be used in educational
- institution for the development of problem solving skills that
- Would be beneficial for student's practical life.
- Generally students follow instructions blindly but metacognitive skills enable a person to think critically, and logically so students must be aware of them.
- Metacognitive skills may be used at very basic level.E.g,
- Childhood by parents so that their children can become good learner.
- Metacognition skills are effective in developing higher order skills. So these skills must be used by students and teacher.
- Self-regulation is useful in achieving directed goals.

CHAPTER 4
REFERENCES

Alexander, P. (1995), Superimposing a situation – specific and domain- specific perspective on an account of self-regulated learning. Singapore: Prentice-Hall.

Anderson, J. (1988). Cognitive Styles and Multicultural Populations, Journal of Teacher Education, retrieved on 15-02-2005 from http:/www.google.com

Anderson, V. & Hidi, S. (1988-1989. Teaching students to summarize Educational Leadership. Retrieved on 15-12-2005 from http://www.proquest.com

Baker, (1982). An Evaluation of the Role of Metacognitive Deficits in learning Disabilities. http:/www.finarticles.com

Bakar, L., & Brown, A.L. (1984). Metacognitive skills and reading. Toronto; Pearson, Ins.

Berks, E.L. (1999). Child Development. New Delhi: Prentice-Hall.

Bouffard-Bouchard, T., & Pinard, A. (1988). Sentiment d'auto efficacite et exercise does processes d'autoregulation chez des estudiants de niveau collegial. Journal International retrieved on December 13, 2005 from: http:/www.psyhinfo.com

Brown, A., Branford, J., Ferrara, R., & Campione, J. (1983). Learning remembering and understanding. New York: Wiley.

Brown, A.I. (1978). Knowing Shen, where and how to remember; A problem of metacognition, New York; Halstead Press.

Carr, M., Borkowski J.G. (1987. The importance of attribution retraining of the generalization of the American Educational Research Association. Retrieved on 01-02-2005 from http//www. Hotbot.com.

Corwley, K., Shrager, J. & Siegler, R.S. (1977). Strategy Discovery as a Competitive Negotiation between Metacognitve and Associative Mechanisms. NY; McGraw Hill.

Crowley, K., Shrager, J. & Siegler, (R.S.) (1997). Strategy Discovery as a Competitive Negotiation between Metacognitive and Associate Mechanisms. Retrieved on 01-12-2005 from http//www. Hotbot.com.

Crowley, K. Shrager, J. < & Siegler, R.S. (1997). Strategy Discovery as a Competitive Negotiation between metacognitive and associative mechanisms. Developmental review, retrieved on 15-10-2005 from http:/wwwfindarticles.com.

Eccles, J.E.Wighfield, A., & Schiefele, U. (1998). Motivation to Succeed. New York;

Ferrari, M. & Mahalingam, R. (1988). Personal cognitive development and its implications for teaching and learning. Toronto. Prentice Hall.

Ferrari, M. & Mahalingam, R. (1998). Personal cognitive development and its implications for teaching and learning. Toronto, Prentice-Hall.

Flavell, 1985. Cognitive Development, NJ Prentice Hall.

Flavell, (1978). Metacognitive Development. London; Alphen a.d. Rijn.

Flavell, J.H. (1979). Metacognition and cognitive monitoring; A new area of cognitive developmental inquiry. Retrieved on 01-12-2005 from http:// www. Hotbot.com

Flvell, J.H. (1999). Cognitive Psychology: US A Wadsworth Publishing Company.

Harter, S. (1982). Processes underlying self-concept formation in children,. Psychological perspectives on the self, NJ: Lawrence Erlbaum Associates.

Hartman, H. (1990). Intelligent Tutoring. Sydney. H & H Publishing Co;

Kazdin, E.(2000) Encyclopedia of Psychology. New York: Oxford University Press.

Langer. E.J. (1989) Mindfulness. Retrieved on 10-11-2005 from http;// www.findarticles.com

Maxwell, M. (1993). Teaching Skills, New York Halstead Press.

Palincsar, A.S. & Brown, A. (1984). Reciprocal teaching of comprehension fostering and comprehension-monitoring activities. Retrieved on December 12,2005 from http;// psychinfo.com.

Pinard, A. (1986),"Prise deconscience" and taking charge of on's cognitive functioning Human Development. Journal. Retrieved on 11-08-2005 from http:// www.Findarticles .com

Pinard, A (1991). Metaconsciousness and Metacognition. NY McGraw-Hill.

Pinard, A. (1991) Metaconsciousness and Metacognition. Allocation addressed to the http;/ www.psychology.com

Pinard, A. (1991). Metaconsciousness and Metacognition. Allocution address to the Canadian psychological Association in Calgary. Alberta.

Santrock W.J. (2001). Adolescence. U.S.A. McGraw Hills.

Sternberg, R.L. (1984). What should intelligence tests test? Implications for a Triarchic theory of intelligence for intelligence testing. Educational Research Journal retrieved on 05 January, 2006 from http;/www/psychinfo.com.

Tauris, C. and Wade, C. (1997). Psychology in Perspective, U.S.A. Educational Publishers.

Veenman, M.V.J., Elshout, J.J. & Meijer (1997). The Generality VS Domin-specificity of Metacognition Skills in Novice Learning Across Domains. NJ. McGraw-Hill.

Westen, D. (1996). Psychology Mind, Brain & Culture. U.S.A. John Wiley & Sons

CPSIA information can be obtained at www.ICGtesting.com
Printed in the USA
LVOW06s1828280314

379396LV00001B/98/P